Symphony No. 9
in D Minor, Op. 125
("Choral")

Ludwig van Beethoven

DOVER PUBLICATIONS, INC.

Mineola, New York

Published in Canada by General Publishing Company, Ltd., 30 Lesmill Road, Don Mills, Toronto, Ontario.

Published in the United Kingdom by Constable and Company, Ltd., 3 The Lanchesters, 162–164 Fulham Palace Road, London W6 9ER.

Bibliographical Note

This Dover edition, first published in 1997, is a republication of music from *Symphonies de Beethoven. Partitions d'Orchestre*, originally published by Henry Litolff's Verlag, Braunschweig, n.d. Lists of contents and instrumentation and notes on the vocal texts are newly added.

International Standard Book Number: 0-486-29924-4

Manufactured in the United States of America
Dover Publications, Inc., 31 East 2nd Street, Mineola, N.Y. 11501

CONTENTS

Dedicated to Friedrich Wilhelm III of Prussia

Symphony No. 9
in D Minor, Op. 125

(1822–24)

Score footnotes:

Page 102, m. 8: In the nature of a recitative, but in tempo
Page 135, mm. 426–431: These six measures may be omitted by the [Tenor]
soloist, but not by the chorus

BEETHOVEN AND
SCHILLER'S *ODE AN DIE FREUDE*

[Beethoven] did not return to Vienna until the last migratory birds had left for the winter; it was already the end of October [1822] . . . The new symphony was finished up to the fourth movement; that is, he had it all in his head and the main ideas were fixed in the sketchbooks. Contrary to his usual method of working, he frequently put the music aside, especially the fourth movement, for he could not decide which verses to choose from Schiller's ode, *An die Freude* . . . The working out of the fourth movement, however, began a struggle seldom encountered before. The problem was to find a suitable introduction to Schiller's ode. One day he burst into the room and shouted at me: 'I have it! I have it!' He held his sketchbook out to me so that I could read: 'Let us sing the song of the immortal Schiller'; then a solo voice began the Hymn to Joy. Yet this introduction must later have given place to another, undeniably more appropriate one:

> *'O friends, not these strains!*
> *Let us sing still more beautifully, still more joyfully!'*

Anton Felix Schindler (1860)

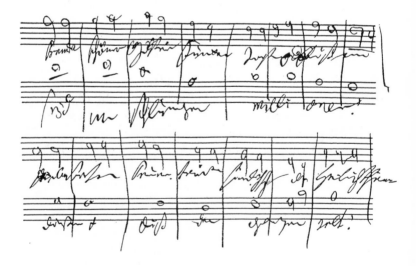

TEXTS

Recitative
(Text by Beethoven)

[p. 113]

O friends, not these strains! Let us sing still more beautifully, still more joyfully!

"Ode to Joy"
(Excerpts from Friedrich Schiller's *Ode an die Freude,* 1785)

[p. 115]

Joy, beautiful divine spark, maiden from Elysium: we are intoxicated with fire, heavenly being, as we enter your sanctuary! Your spells reunite what fashion has rigidly sundered: all men become brothers wherever your gentle wing reposes.

Let whoever has gained the great stake and has become a friend of a friend, whoever has won a lovely woman, let him add his jubilation to ours! Yes, whoever in the world merely calls a soul his own! And let whoever has never been able to do so, let him steal away in tears from this company.

All beings drink joy at the breasts of nature; all good men, all evil men, follow her trail of roses. She gave us kisses and the vine, a friend tested in death; ecstacy was granted to the worm, and the cherub stands in the sight of God!

[p. 131]

Happily as His suns fly through heaven's splendid field, brothers, run your course joyfully as a hero to victory . . .

[p. 146]

Be embraced, O millions! This kiss for the whole world! Brothers! a loving Father must dwell above the starry tent. You fall down, O millions? Do you have a presentiment of the Creator, O world? Seek Him above the starry tent! He must dwell over stars . . . .

- Schindler's narrative is excerpted from
  Beethoven As I Knew Him, Dover, 1996 (0-486-29232-0).
- Beethoven's score sketch is a facsimile of the autograph of 1823
  for the beginning of the last movement of Symphony No. 9.
- The English translation of the Schiller excerpts
  was prepared specially for this edition.

INSTRUMENTATION

Piccolo [Flauto piccolo]
2 Flutes [Flauti, Fl.]
2 Oboes [Oboi, Ob.]
2 Clarinets in C, A, B♭("B") [Clarinetti, Cl.]
2 Bassoons [Fagotti, Fag.]
Contrabassoon [Contrafagotto, Ctr. Fag.]

4 Horns in D, E♭("Es"), B♭("B"), B♭-basso
    [Corni, Cor.]
2 Trumpets in D, B♭("B") [Tromba/e, Tr.]
3 Trombones [Tromboni, Tb(i). (Alto, Tenore, Basso)]

Timpani [Timpani, Tp.]

Percussion
    Triangle [Triangolo]
    Cymbals [Cinelli]
    Bass Drum [Gran Tamburo]

Violins I, II [Violino]
Violas [Viola]

    Solo Vocal Quartet
        (Soprano, Alto, Tenor, Bass-Baritone)
    Mixed Chorus (SATB)

Cellos [Violoncello,Vcl.]
Basses [Basso/i]

Symphony No. 9
in D Minor, Op. 125
("Choral")

Symphony No. 9

in D Minor, Op. 125

("Choral")

1

2

20

31

40

49

54

74

104

110

nehmere an - stimmen, und freu - - - - - - denvollere.

wir be-tre-ten feu-er-trunken, Himmlische,dein Hei-ligthum! Dei-ne Zauber bin-den wieder,was die Mode streng getheilt;al-

- - le Menschen werden Brü-der, wo dein sanfter Flü-gel weilt.

Deine Zauber binden wieder, was die Mo-de streng getheilt; al -

Deine Zauber binden wieder, was die Mo-de streng getheilt; al -

Deine Zauber binden wieder, was die Mo-de streng getheilt; al -

118

- - le Menschen werden Brüder, wo dein sanfter Flügel weilt.

- - le Menschen werden Brüder, wo dein sanfter Flügel weilt.

- - le Menschen werden Brüder, wo dein sanfter Flügel weilt.

122

124

uns und Re - ben, ei - nen Freund ge - prüft im Tod, Wol - - lust ward dem Wurm ge - ge - ben,

uns und Re - ben, ei - nen Freund ge - prüft im Tod, Wol - - lust ward dem Wurm ge - ge - ben,

uns und Re - ben, ei - nen Freund ge - prüft im Tod, Wol - - lust ward dem Wurm ge - ge - ben,

uns und Re - ben, ei - nen Freund ge - prüft im Tod, Wol - - lust ward dem Wurm ge - ge - ben,

311

126

ALLA MARCIA.
331
Allegro assai vivace. 𝅗𝅥 = 84.
Flauto piccolo.
Flauti.
Oboi.
Clarinetti in B.
Fagotti.
Contrafagotto.
Corni in D.
Corni in B.
Tromba I in D.
Tromba II in B.
Timpani.
Triangolo.
Cinelli.
Gran Tamburo.
Violino I.
Violino II.
Viola.
Tenore Solo.
Tenore I.
Tenore II.
Bassi.
CORO.
Violoncello, e Basso.
pp

356
sempre pp
sempre pp
sempre pp
sempre pp
sempre pp
sempre pp
sempre pp
sempre pp
sempre pp
pp
pp
pp
pp

froh, wie sei_ne Son_nen flie_gen durch des Himmels prächt'_gen Plan, lau_fet, Brü_der, eu_re Bahn, lau_fet,

Brü_der, eu_re Bahn,— freu_dig, wie ein Held zum Sie_gen, wie ein Held____ zum Sie_gen, lau_fet, Brü_der,

Nr.(Diese 6 Takte können nicht vom Chor, wohl aber vom Solosänger ausgelassen werden) *

zum Sie—gen, freu_dig, freu_dig wie ein Held, ein Held zum Sie-gen.

zum Sie-gen, freu_dig, freu dig wie ein Held zum Sie - gen.

zum Sie-gen, freu_dig, freu dig wie ein Held zum Sie - gen.

zum Sie_gen, freu_dig, freu_dig wie ein Held zum Sie - gen.

144

weilt; dei _ ne Zau _ ber bin _ den wie _ der, was die Mo _ de streng ge _ theilt; al _ _ le Men_schen

weilt; dei _ ne Zau _ ber bin _ den wie _ der, was die Mo _ de streng ge _ theilt; al _ _ le Men_schen

weilt; dei _ ne Zau _ ber bin _ den wie _ der, was die Mo _ de streng ge _ theilt; al _ le Men _ schen

weilt; dei _ ne Zau _ ber bin _ den wie _ der, was die Mo _ de streng ge _ theilt; al _ le Men_schen

146

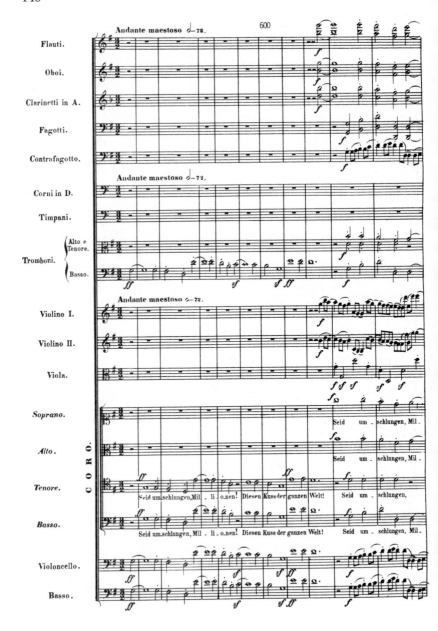

152

164

733
p cresc.
p cresc.
p cresc.
cresc.
cresc.
cresc.
cresc.
Such ihn ü - berm Ster - nen zelt,
p
Ah - nest du den Schö - pfer, Welt!
o - nen?
cresc.
cresc.

754

763
Allegro ma non tanto. 𝅗𝅥 = 120.
Flauto piccolo.
Flauti.
Oboi.
Clarinetti.
Fagotti.
Contrafagotto.
Corni.
Allegro ma non tanto. 𝅗𝅥 = 120.
Corni.
Trombe.
Timpani.
Tromboni.
Alto e Tenore.
Basso.
Violino I. II.
Viola.
sempre pp
Allegro ma non tanto. 𝅗𝅥 = 120.
SOLI.
Soprano.
Alto.
Tenore.
Basso.
Freu - de, Tochter aus E -
CORO.
Soprano.
Alto.
Tenore.
Basso.
Violoncello e Basso.

Freu - de, Tochter aus E - ly - si - um!

Freu - de Tochter aus E - ly - si - um

ly - si - um!

777
Fl.I.
Ob.I.
pp
II.
I.
I.
II.
pp
sempre pp
sempre pp
pizz.
pizz.
pizz.
Toch - ter, Tochter aus E - ly - sium!
Dei - ne Zauber, deine Zauber
Toch - ter, Tochter aus E - ly - sium!
Deine Zauber, deine Zauber
Toch - ter, Tochter aus E - ly - sium!
Deine Zauber,
Toch - ter, Tochter aus E - ly - sium!

811

wie_der, was die Mo_de streng ge_theilt.   Al _ _ le Menschen, al _ le

wie_der, was die Mo_de streng ge_theilt.   Al _ _ le Menschen, al _ le

wie_der, was die Mo_de streng ge_theilt.   Al _ _ le Menschen, al _ le

wie_der, was die Mo_de streng ge_theilt.   Al _ _ le Menschen, al _ le

836

841
Poco Allegro, stringendo il tempo, sempre più Allegro.
cresc.
Poco Allegro, stringendo il tempo, sempre più Allegro.
cresc.
Poco Allegro, stringendo il tempo, sempre più Allegro.
pp
cresc.
Flügel weilt.
Flügel weilt.
weilt.
Flügel weilt.
pp
cresc.

902
a 2.
a 2.
a 2.
zen
Welt!
Freude,
Freude, schöner
Göt - ter - funken!
schöner

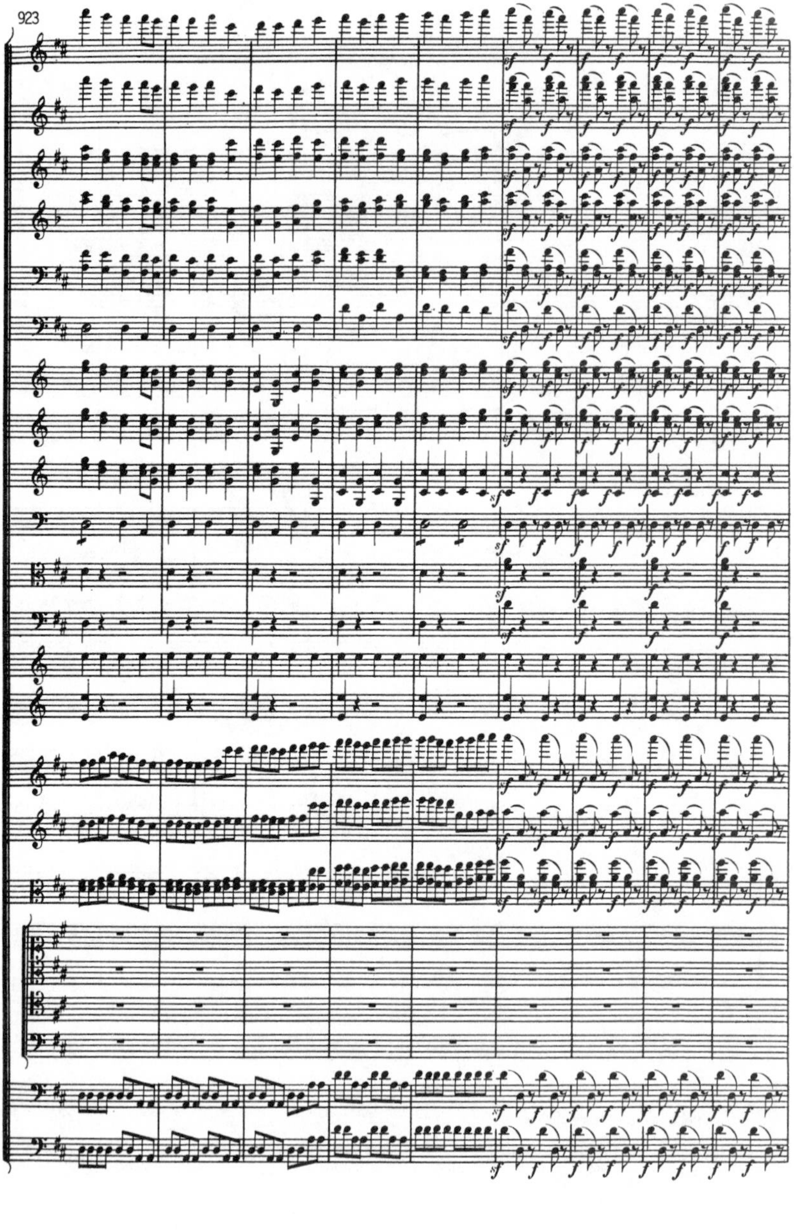
923

END OF EDITION

DOVER FULL-SIZE ORCHESTRAL SCORES

THE SIX BRANDENBURG CONCERTOS AND THE FOUR ORCHESTRAL SUITES IN FULL SCORE, Johann Sebastian Bach. Complete standard Bach-Gesellschaft editions in large, clear format. Study score. 273pp. 9 × 12. 23376-6 Pa. **$11.95**

COMPLETE CONCERTI FOR SOLO KEYBOARD AND OR-CHESTRA IN FULL SCORE, Johann Sebastian Bach. Bach's seven complete concerti for solo keyboard and orchestra in full score from the authoritative Bach-Gesellschaft edition. 206pp. 9 × 12.
24929-8 Pa. **$11.95**

THE THREE VIOLIN CONCERTI IN FULL SCORE, Johann Sebastian Bach. Concerto in A Minor, BWV 1041; Concerto in E Major, BWV 1042; and Concerto for Two Violins in D Minor, BWV 1043. Bach-Gesellschaft edition. 64pp. 9⅜ × 12¼. 25124-1 Pa. **$6.95**

GREAT ORGAN CONCERTI, OPP. 4 & 7, IN FULL SCORE, George Frideric Handel. 12 organ concerti composed by great Baroque master are reproduced in full score from the *Deutsche Handelgesell-schaft* edition. 138pp. 9⅜ × 12¼. 24462-8 Pa. **$8.95**

COMPLETE CONCERTI GROSSI IN FULL SCORE, George Frideric Handel. Monumental Opus 6 Concerti Grossi, Opus 3 and "Alexander's Feast" Concerti Grossi—19 in all—reproduced from most authoritative edition. 258pp. 9⅜ × 12¼. 24187-4 Pa. **$13.95**

LATER SYMPHONIES, Wolfgang A. Mozart. Full orchestral scores to last symphonies (Nos. 35–41) reproduced from definitive Breitkopf & Härtel Complete Works edition. Study score. 285pp. 9 × 12.
23052-X Pa. **$12.95**

PIANO CONCERTOS NOS. 17–22, Wolfgang Amadeus Mozart. Six complete piano concertos in full score, with Mozart's own cadenzas for Nos. 17–19. Breitkopf & Härtel edition. Study score. 370pp. 9⅜ × 12¼.
23599-8 Pa. **$16.95**

PIANO CONCERTOS NOS. 23–27, Wolfgang Amadeus Mozart. Mozart's last five piano concertos in full score, plus cadenzas for Nos. 23 and 27, and the Concert Rondo in D Major, K.382. Breitkopf & Härtel edition. Study score. 310pp. 9⅜ × 12¼. 23600-5 Pa. **$13.95**

CONCERTI FOR WIND INSTRUMENTS IN FULL SCORE, Wolfgang Amadeus Mozart. Exceptional volume contains ten pieces for orchestra and wind instruments and includes some of Mozart's finest, most popular music. 272pp. 9⅜ × 12¼.   25228-0 Pa. **$13.95**

SYMPHONIES 88–92 IN FULL SCORE: The Haydn Society Edition, Joseph Haydn. Full score of symphonies Nos. 88 through 92. Large, readable noteheads, ample margins for fingerings, etc., and extensive Editor's Commentary. 304pp. 9 × 12. (Available in U.S. only)
24445-8 Pa. **$15.95**

THE RITE OF SPRING IN FULL SCORE, Igor Stravinsky. A reprint of the original full-score edition of the most famous musical work of the 20th century, created as a ballet score for Diaghilev's Ballets Russes. 176pp. 9⅜ × 12¼. (Available in U.S. only)   25857-2 Pa. **$9.95**

FOUR SYMPHONIES IN FULL SCORE, Franz Schubert. Schubert's four most popular symphonies: No. 4 in C Minor ("Tragic"); No. 5 in B-flat Major; No. 8 in B Minor ("Unfinished"); and No. 9 in C Major ("Great"). Breitkopf & Härtel edition. Study score. 261pp. 9⅜ × 12¼.
23681-1 Pa. **$13.95**

GREAT OVERTURES IN FULL SCORE, Carl Maria von Weber. Overtures to *Oberon, Der Freischutz,Euryanthe* and *Preciosa* reprinted from auhoritative Breitkopf & Härtel editions. 112pp. 9 × 12.
25225-6 Pa. **$9.95**

SYMPHONIES NOS. 1, 2, 3, AND 4 IN FULL SCORE, Ludwig van Beethoven. Republication of H. Litolff edition. 272pp. 9 × 12.
26033-X Pa. $11.95

SYMPHONIES NOS. 5, 6 AND 7 IN FULL SCORE, Ludwig van Beethoven. Republication of the H. Litolff edition. 272pp. 9 × 12.
26034-8 Pa. **$11.95**

SYMPHONIES NOS. 8 AND 9 IN FULL SCORE, Ludwig van Beethoven. Republication of the H. Litolff edition. 256pp. 9 × 12.
26035-6 Pa. **$11.95**

SIX GREAT OVERTURES IN FULL SCORE, Ludwig van Beethoven. Six staples of the orchestral repertoire from authoritative Breitkopf & Härtel edition. *Leonore Overtures*, Nos. 1–3; Overtures to *Coriolanus, Egmont, Fidelio.* 288pp. 9 × 12.   24789-9 Pa. **$13.95**

COMPLETE PIANO CONCERTOS IN FULL SCORE, Ludwig van Beethoven. Complete scores of five great Beethoven piano concertos, with all cadenzas as he wrote them, reproduced from authoritative Breitkopf & Härtel edition. New table of contents. 384pp. 9⅜ × 12¼.
24563-2 Pa. **$15.95**

GREAT ROMANTIC VIOLIN CONCERTI IN FULL SCORE, Ludwig van Beethoven, Felix Mendelssohn and Peter Ilyitch Tchaikovsky. The Beethoven Op. 61, Mendelssohn, Op. 64 and Tchaikovsky, Op. 35 concertos reprinted from the Breitkopf & Härtel editions. 224pp. 9 × 12.   24989-1 Pa. **$10.95**

MAJOR ORCHESTRAL WORKS IN FULL SCORE, Felix Mendelssohn. Generally considered to be Mendelssohn's finest orchestral works, here in one volume are: the complete *Midsummer Night's Dream; Hebrides Overture; Calm Sea and Prosperous Voyage Overture;* Symphony No. 3 in A ("Scottish"); and Symphony No. 4 in A ("Italian"). Breitkopf & Härtel edition. Study score. 406pp. 9 × 12.

23184-4 Pa. **$18.95**

COMPLETE SYMPHONIES, Johannes Brahms. Full orchestral scores. No. 1 in C Minor, Op. 68; No. 2 in D Major, Op. 73; No. 3 in F Major, Op. 90; and No. 4 in E Minor, Op. 98. Reproduced from definitive Vienna Gesellschaft der Musikfreunde edition. Study score. 344pp. 9 × 12.   23053-8 Pa. **$14.95**

THE VIOLIN CONCERTI AND THE SINFONIA CONCERTANTE, K.364, IN FULL SCORE, Wolfgang Amadeus Mozart. All five violin concerti and famed double concerto reproduced from authoritative Breitkopf & Härtel Complete Works Edition. 208pp. 9⅜ × 12½.   25169-1 Pa. **$12.95**

17 DIVERTIMENTI FOR VARIOUS INSTRUMENTS, Wolfgang A. Mozart. Sparkling pieces of great vitality and brilliance from 1771-1779; consecutively numbered from 1 to 17. Reproduced from definitive Breitkopf & Härtel Complete Works edition. Study score. 241pp. 9⅜ × 12¼.   23862-8 Pa. **$13.95**

WATER MUSIC AND MUSIC FOR THE ROYAL FIREWORKS IN FULL SCORE, George Frideric Handel. Full scores of two of the most popular Baroque orchestral works performed today—reprinted from definitive Deutsche Handelgesellschaft edition. Total of 96pp. 8⅛ × 11.

25070-9 Pa. **$7.95**

FOURTH, FIFTH AND SIXTH SYMPHONIES IN FULL SCORE, Peter Ilyitch Tchaikovsky. Complete orchestral scores of Symphony No. 4 in F minor, Op. 36; Symphony No. 5 in E minor, Op. 64; Symphony No. 6 in B minor, "Pathetique," Op. 74. Study score. Breitkopf & Härtel editions. 480pp. 9⅜ × 12¼.   23861-X Pa. **$19.95**

ROMEO AND JULIET OVERTURE AND CAPRICCIO ITALIEN IN FULL SCORE, Peter Ilyitch Tchaikovsky. Two of Russian master's most popular compositions in high quality, inexpensive reproduction. From authoritative Russian edition. 208pp. 8⅜ × 11½.

25217-5 Pa. **$10.95**

COMPLETE CONCERTI GROSSI IN FULL SCORE, Arcangelo Corelli. All 12 concerti in the famous late nineteenth-century edition prepared by violinist Joseph Joachim and musicologist Friedrich Chrysander. 240pp. 8⅜ × 11¼. 25606-5 Pa. **$12.95**

PIANO CONCERTOS NOS. 11–16 IN FULL SCORE, Wolfgang Amadeus Mozart. Authoritative Breitkopf & Härtel edition of six staples of the concerto repertoire, including Mozart's cadenzas for Nos. 12–16. 256pp. 9⅜ × 12¼. 25468-2 Pa. **$12.95**

NUTCRACKER SUITE IN FULL SCORE, Peter Ilyitch Tchaikovsky. Among the most popular ballet pieces ever created—a complete, inexpensive, high-quality score to study and enjoy. 128pp. 9 × 12. 25379-1 Pa. **$8.95**

TONE POEMS, SERIES I: DON JUAN, TOD UND VERKLARUNG, and DON QUIXOTE, Richard Strauss. Three of the most often performed and recorded works in entire orchestral repertoire, reproduced in full score from original editions. Study score. 286pp. 9⅜ × 12¼. (Available in U.S. only) 23754-0 Pa. **$13.95**

TONE POEMS, SERIES II: TILL EULENSPIEGELS LUSTIGE STREICHE, ALSO SPRACH ZARATHUSTRA, and EIN HELDENLEBEN, Richard Strauss. Three important orchestral works, including very popular *Till Eulenspiegel's Merry Pranks,* reproduced in full score from original editions. Study score. 315pp. 9⅜ × 12¼. (Available in U.S. only) 23755-9 Pa. **$14.95**

DAS LIED VON DER ERDE IN FULL SCORE, Gustav Mahler. Mahler's masterpiece, a fusion of song and symphony, reprinted from the original 1912 Universal Edition. English translations of song texts. 160pp. 9 × 12. 25657-X Pa. **$9.95**

SYMPHONIES NOS. 1 AND 2 IN FULL SCORE, Gustav Mahler. Unabridged, authoritative Austrian editions of Symphony No. 1 in D Major ("Titan") and Symphony No. 2 in C Minor ("Resurrection"). 384pp. 8⅛ × 11. 25473-9 Pa. **$14.95**

SYMPHONIES NOS. 3 AND 4 IN FULL SCORE, Gustav Mahler. Two brilliantly contrasting masterworks—one scored for a massive ensemble, the other for small orchestra and soloist—reprinted from authoritative Viennese editions. 368pp. 9⅜ × 12¼. 26166-2 Pa. **$16.95**

SYMPHONY NO. 8 IN FULL SCORE, Gustav Mahler. Superb authoritative edition of massive, complex "Symphony of a Thousand." Scored for orchestra, eight solo voices, double chorus, boys' choir and organ. Reprint of Izdatel'stvo "Muzyka," Moscow, edition. Translation of texts. 272pp. 9⅜ × 12¼. 26022-4 Pa. **$12.95**

DAPHNIS AND CHLOE IN FULL SCORE, Maurice Ravel. Definitive full-score edition of Ravel's rich musical setting of a Greek fable by Longus is reprinted here from the original French edition. 320pp. 9⅜ × 12¼. (Not available in France or Germany)   25826-2¹ Pa. **$15.95**

THREE GREAT ORCHESTRAL WORKS IN FULL SCORE, Claude Debussy. Three favorites by influential modernist: *Prélude à l'Après-midi d'un Faune, Nocturnes,* and *La Mer.* Reprinted from early French editions. 279pp. 9 × 12.   24441-5 Pa. **$13.95**

SYMPHONY IN D MINOR IN FULL SCORE, César Franck. Superb, authoritative edition of Franck's only symphony, an often-performed and recorded masterwork of late French romantic style. 160pp. 9 × 12.   25373-2 Pa. **$9.95**

THE GREAT WALTZES IN FULL SCORE, Johann Strauss, Jr. Complete scores of eight melodic masterpieces: The Beautiful Blue Danube, Emperor Waltz, Tales of the Vienna Woods, Wiener Blut, four more. Authoritative editions. 336pp. 8⅜ × 11¼.   26009-7 Pa. **$14.95**

THE FIREBIRD IN FULL SCORE (Original 1910 Version), Igor Stravinsky. Handsome, inexpensive edition of modern masterpiece, renowned for brilliant orchestration, glowing color. Authoritative Russian edition. 176pp. 9⅜ × 12¼. (Available in U.S. only)   25535-2 Pa. **$10.95**

PETRUSHKA IN FULL SCORE: Original Version, Igor Stravinsky. The definitive full-score edition of Stravinsky's masterful score for the great Ballets Russes 1911 production of *Petrushka.* 160pp. 9⅜ × 12¼. (Available in U.S. only)   25680-4 Pa. **$9.95**
